HEROIC HORSES

Written by Emily Kington

CONTENTS

Horses	4
Wild and Free	6
Horses and Humans	8
Horse Power	10
Farm Horses	12
Police Horses	14
Horse Breeds	16
Little and Large	18
Race Horses	20
Eventing	22
Rodeo	24
More Horse Sports	26
Grooming & Equipment	28
Learning to Ride	30
Glossary	31
Index	32

First published in 2024 by
Hungry Tomato Ltd
F15, Old Bakery Studios,
Blewetts Wharf, Malpas Road,
Truro, Cornwall,
TR1 1QH, UK.

Thanks to our editor, Julie Tofflemire.

Copyright © 2024 Hungry Tomato Ltd

No part of this publication may be reproduced, stored in a retrieval system, or transmitted in any form or by any means, electronic, mechanical, photocopying, recording, or otherwise, without prior written permission of the copyright owner.

A CIP catalogue record for this book is available from the British Library.

ISBN 9781835691182
Printed in China

Discover more at
www.hungrytomato.com

Neither the publisher nor the author shall be liable for any bodily harm or damage to property whatsoever that may be caused or sustained as a result of conducting any of the activities featured in this book.

DISCLAIMER:
The activities featured in this book have been carried out by trained professionals and experiences horse riders. Do not try them yourself or approach horses without supervision.

All words in **BOLD** can be found in the glossary.

HORSES

Horses are fast, strong and beautiful. A horse galloping across a field will make people stop and watch until the show is over!

These gentle creatures have had a special connection to humans for thousands of years.

Horses are very powerful. We use the word "horsepower" to measure the power of our cars. We compare a car's power against the natural power of a horse.

WILD AND FREE

Most horses need care from humans, but some still live in the wild on their own.

Przewalski's (pronounced *shuh-VAL-skeez*) horses mainly live in the grasslands of Mongolia. They are called "takhi" by Mongolians. For food, the horses **graze** on grass and leaves.

THERE ARE ABOUT 2,000 OF THESE HORSES LEFT IN THE WILD.

Przewalski's horses

Scientists believe that there are no truly wild horses left. The free-roaming horses we see today come from **domesticated** horses that had escaped back into the wild.

Corolla wild horses in North Carolina, USA

HORSES AND HUMANS

Horses have been important to humans for a long time.

About 6,000 years ago, people started to **tame** horses. Groups of people that had domesticated horses were faster and stronger than groups that didn't.

Horses helped people travel farther and for longer periods of time. Once the wheel was invented, horses could pull big loads.

A 15,000-year-old cave painting from France

Terracotta (clay) statues from the late 200s BCE were found in China.

In the Middle Ages (around CE 500 to 1500), knights rode war horses into battle. A war horse was very expensive. It cost as much as a new car does today! War horses were trained to kick and bite their knight's enemies.

Knights competed in jousting competitions too. They tried to knock each other from their horses using long lances.

A modern-day display of jousting

Knight

Lance

HORSE POWER

In the past, horses provided power for our heavy machines. They pulled farm machines and fire engines.

Fire horses pull a fire engine in New York City, USA, around 1910.

Harness

Steam-powered pump to spray the water

When the fire bells rang, experienced fire horses would leave their stalls and stand ready under their harnesses.

The cavalry were army units that used the power of horses. There were two kinds of cavalry. The light cavalry carried riders into battle.

Light cavalry horses

The heavy cavalry pulled cannons. They also carried soldiers in wagons to the battlefields. Today, we use jeeps, trucks and tanks to do these jobs.

Heavy cavalry horses pulled cannons like these into battle.

FARM HORSES

Many small farms still use horse power today. There are many benefits to using horses on farms.

Horses are more "green" than tractors and oil-powered machines. Horses can refuel off the land by eating grass and hay.

Their **manure** is a good **fertiliser** that helps more crops to grow!

A horse-drawn plough in 1904

A horse pulling a plough in more modern times

When cutting wood in old forests, some people still use horses to remove logs. Horses are low impact compared to machines. This means they don't damage the ground or hurt plants and wildlife.

A workhorse for logging

POLICE HORSES

Big cities have police officers mounted on horses. They can be more useful than police cars.

Officers on horseback can see out over crowds. Police horses can go places cars can't go, such as alleyways and through traffic jams.

Police horses need to be calm and steady. They are trained for 6 to 18 months.

A police horse in training

Sometimes police officers need to go into a rough area of land. Horses can go anywhere the criminal goes – and faster!

The Texas Rangers in the USA use horses. So do the Royal Canadian Mounted Police, or "Mounties".

Mounties have been working in Canada since 1873.

HORSE BREEDS

There are over 500 **breeds** of horses. They have different features and uses.

THOROUGHBRED HORSE

The Thoroughbred breed started in England.

Thoroughbreds were **bred** to be racehorses. Horses that won races were bred with other winners so that each **generation** became faster.

Foal

A THOROUGHBRED RACEHORSE CAN RUN FASTER THAN 40 MPH!

QUARTER HORSE

Quarter horses were bred in America for racing and working with cattle. If running over 400 metres or less, quarter horses are faster than any other horses in the world.

ARABIAN HORSE

Arabian horses originally came from **Arabia**. They were bred to live in the hot, dry desert. Their coats are fine and silky to help them get rid of heat more easily.

LITTLE AND LARGE

Horses come in all sizes, from tiny to gigantic.

MEASURING HORSES

- Horses and ponies are measured in "hands". A hand is 10.16 cm.
- Horses are measured from the ground to the top of their withers.
- Horse are 14 hands 5 cm tall, or taller.
- Ponies are shorter than 14 hands 5 cm.

The world's smallest foal is just 23 cm tall!

Withers

Some of the biggest breeds in the world are Belgian draught horses and Shires. On average, these enormous creatures can grow up to 16 to 17 hands tall (163–173 cm). Some grow even bigger!

These gentle giants are patient and follow instructions well.

DRAUGHT HORSES ARE STRONG AND MUSCULAR HORSES BRED TO PULL HEAVY LOADS.

RACE HORSES

Horses have become an important part of our hobbies and entertainment. Horses are used in many sports, such as racing.

On average, a racehorse can run 40 to 44 mph. From a standing start, a racehorse can cover a 100 metres in just over 5 seconds!

EVENTING

Eventing is a sport that includes three different tests for a horse and rider.

The sport grew out of the tests that were used to train cavalry riders and their horses.

TEST 1: DRESSAGE

The horse must move in straight lines and perfect circles. It must stop exactly on spots marked by big letters.

A horse participates in a dressage test.

TEST 2: CROSS-COUNTRY

The horse and rider gallop across the countryside taking jumps. They must do this in a set time. Each minute of overtime loses the rider points.

Brush fence

TEST 3: SHOW-JUMPING / STADIUM JUMPING

The horse must jump a series of **obstacles** in order. There is a **penalty** for knocking down an obstacle.

Vertical jumps

RODEO

Rodeo is a popular sport that grew out of ranch work. Cowboys and their horses would compete to show off their skills.

"Cutting" is when the rider and horse work together to safely separate a cow from the herd.

Cowhorses are bred to have "cow sense". This means that they can tell in advance how the cows will move.

Cutting

When a cow is away from the herd, it can be roped for **branding** or **vaccinations**. Horses used for roping need to have good speed and be able to stop quickly.

Roping

Barrel racing shows both speed and **agility**, something cowhorses need. The horses must gallop around the barrels without knocking them over.

Barrel racing

Barrel

MORE HORSE SPORTS

Horses are a part of other popular sports around the world, and this has been true throughout history!

Chariot races in Greece date back to 700 BCE. The sport was very dangerous for both the horses and the riders.

A modern display of chariot races

Chariot

In modern carriage driving trials, horses must complete a series of challenges. These include a race with gates called "hazards".

Hazard

In polo, players on horseback try to hit a wooden ball between two goalposts. They use mallets with long handles.

Mallet

GROOMING & EQUIPMENT

Horses need a lot of care and equipment.

Grooming is one way to keep a horse healthy and create a friendship with it. Grooming means cleaning and brushing the horse.

The horse is first brushed with a curry comb and a body brush to get the dirt and loose hair off. Then a soft brush is used to remove the final dust and make the coat shiny.

Soft brush

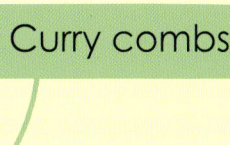

Curry combs

The equipment used for riding a horse is called "tack".

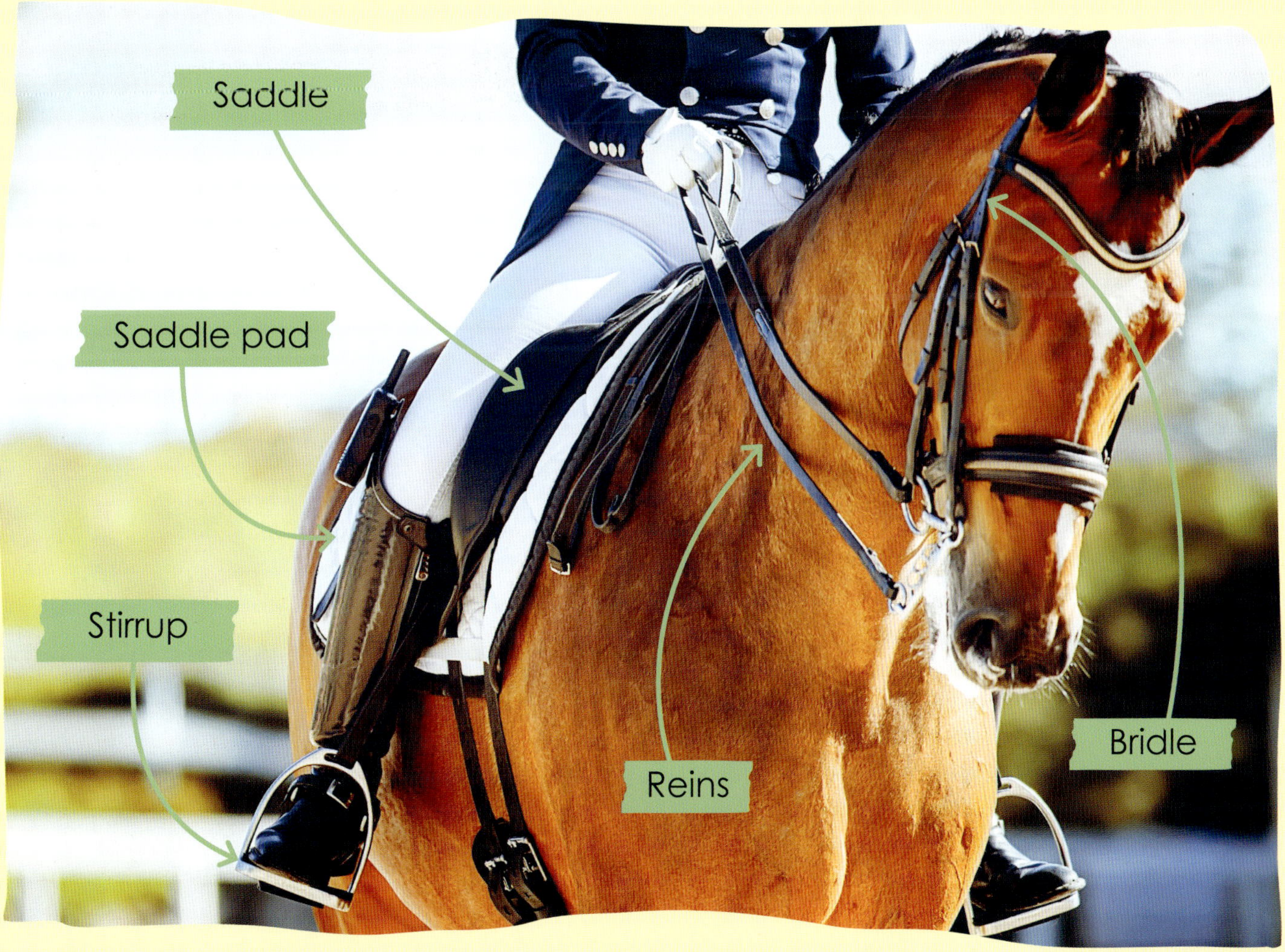

Saddle

Saddle pad

Stirrup

Reins

Bridle

LEARNING TO RIDE

Do you want to learn to ride or drive horses? Search online to find riding schools.

Visit several places before you make up your mind.
Watch some lessons and ask yourself these questions:

- Are safety rules followed? Look for people wearing helmets and riding boots.

- Is the teacher nice to the students and the horses?

- Do the horses look well taken care of?

- Is the place tidy?

All these things are important if you want to be safe and have fun.

GLOSSARY

agility – being able to move, and change position, easily and with speed.

Arabia – the area that today is known as the Middle East.

branding – to put a mark on an animal to show who owns it.

bred – (to breed) when a male and female animal are put together by humans so that they mate and have young.

breeds – small groups of animals within a species that all share the same (or very similar) appearance and characteristics. Thoroughbred and Arabian are examples of two different horse breeds.

domesticated – adapted over time from a wild animal to one that can live with humans.

fertiliser – a substance, such as animal manure (see right), that feeds the soil and makes it better for growing crops.

generation – a group of people or animals who are born and live at the same time.

graze – to eat grass and plants in a field or meadow.

manure – animal waste (poop) that is often used by farmers to improve soil.

mounted – sitting on or riding a horse.

obstacles – objects that are in the way.

penalty – a punishment for breaking a rule or law.

ranch – a large farm where animals, such as cattle and sheep, are bred and raised.

tame – to make a wild animal friendly and not afraid of humans. A tame animal can be trained.

vaccinations – injections that contain a substance that will stop a person or animal catching an illness.

INDEX

A
Arabian horses 17

B
barrel racing 25
breeding of horses 16-17, 19, 24
breeds (of horse) 16-17, 19

C
carriage driving 26
cavalry horses 11, 22
chariot races 26
cowboys 24-25
cowhorses 24-25
cross-country events 23
cutting 24

D
draught horse 19
dressage 22

E
equipment (see tack)
eventing 22-23

F
farm horses 10, 12-13
fire horses 10

G
grooming 28-29

H
hands (unit of measurement) 18
history of horses 8-9, 26
horsepower 5
horses in art 8

J
jousting 9

K
knights 9

L
logging 13

M
Mounties (see Royal Canadian Mounted Police)

P
ploughs 12
police horses 14-15
polo 27
Przewalski's horses 6

Q
quarter horses 17

R
racehorses 16, 20-21
riding lessons 30
rodeos 24-25
roping 25
Royal Canadian Mounted Police 15

S
Shire horse 19
show-jumping/stadium jumping 23

T
tack 28-29
Texas Rangers 15
Thoroughbred horses 16

W
war horses 9
wild horses 6-7

Picture credits:
(t=top; b=bottom; m=middle; l=left; r=right):
Shutterstock: Abramova Kseniya 18tr; Azahara Perez 4-5bg; Begir 26m; Callipso88 17br; Dala A Stork 24bg; 25b; Everett Collection 10m, 12tr; Fedor Selivanov 8br; GeptaYs 21t; Gorloff-KV 30b; Jackson Stock Photography 25tr; Jaco wild 17m; Jim Lambert 19m; Karl Aage Isaksen 11b; Keith Tarrier 11t; Kento35 27bg; Krysja 14br; Margo Harrison 23br; Nina Dorozhinskaya 16b; Novikov Aleksey 14m; Olgaru79 23m; Ondrej Prosicky 6-7bg; Pic Media Aus 9bg; Prestigious pHotos 7ml; Rita_Kochmarjova 1bg; Rolf Dannenberg 22b; Samantha Fletcher 29tl; SeventyFour 28bg; Shawn Hamilton 18b; Shona Branigan 13bg; Smereka 12b; Spatuletail 8bl; StaceyL 15bg; Stefan Holm 20-21bg, 31b; Uzo Borewicz 26br; Valeri Vatel 29b; Zhangyuqiu 2-3bg.

Every effort has been made to trace the copyright holders, and we apologise in advance for any unintentional omissions. We would be pleased to insert the appropriate acknowledgements in any subsequent edition of this publication.